SOCIAL MEDIA TRENDS

TECHNOLOGY REVIEW
2023

Preface:

As we enter the year 2023, the influence of social media on our lives has become even more predominant and pervasive than ever before. From the way we communicate, connect, and consume information to the way we conduct business and participate in politics, social media has irrevocably transformed our world in profound ways.

As a result, understanding the complex dynamics of social media and its impact on our society has never been more important. That is why this report on social media in 2023 is so timely and essential.

In this report, we have gathered insights and data from experts in various fields to provide a comprehensive and up-to-date analysis of social media in 2023, we have also gathered online information. We explore the latest trends, challenges, and opportunities in social media, including the rise of new platforms, the evolution of existing ones, and the changing ways in which people use and engage with social media.

We also delve into the impact of social media on key areas of our lives, including politics, business, health, and culture. With a focus on the ethical and social implications of social media, this report aims to provide a nuanced and balanced understanding of this powerful force in our world.

Whether you are a student, researcher, business professional, or concerned citizen, this report on social media in 2023 is an invaluable resource for anyone seeking to understand the current state and future trajectory of this rapidly evolving phenomenon.

We hope that this report will spark thoughtful discussion and debate, as well as inspire further research and exploration, as we continue to grapple with the complex and multifaceted impact of social media on our society.

This book is dedicated to My

Loving Husband Prabhakar Kasu

And

My Adorable son Aryan Kasu

Content

1. Chapter 1 - Introduction to social media

2. Chapter 2 - Industry Reports and Studies

3. Chapter 3 - Social media and Mental Health

4. Chapter 4 - Pros and Cons of social media

5. Chapter 5 - Social media and Youth

6. Chapter 6 - Social media and Marketing

7. Chapter 7 - Social media & Personal Branding

8. Chapter 8 - Social media and Business

9. Chapter 9 – Social media and Privacy

10. Chapter 10 – Conclusion

Chapter – 1

Introduction to Social Media

The impact of social media on people has been both positive and negative. Social media is a technology with a lot of wonderful benefits, it allows people to share and connect, get news and information, and even know new people online. Social media also provides a convenient way for people to stay connected with friends and family at every point and stage of life. Social media played an important role during pandemic and helped lot of families reach out to their families and entertained them. It also allowed for the dissemination of information and the sharing of news & ideas on the global scale.

However, there were negative impacts to of social media too, with addictive and polarizing content, that lead to distorted perception of reality and the spread of echo chambers. In social network, when users engage with like-minded peers and their selective opinions, it results in echo chambers. Social media echo chambers create echo effect where opinions and information are aligned to an ideology or power structure. Social media at times may limit the exposure to diverse perspectives and favours formation of groups of like-minded users framing and reinforcing a shared narrative. It eliminates opposing viewpoints and differing voices, by enforcing the readers or users with biased and tailor-made experience. So, you may be exposed to just one side of the story or opinion.

These echo chambers not only lead to partisan and ideological polarization, but they divide citizens based on their level of support systems. Some of the echo chambers examples could be Internet media, filter bubbles, broadcast media, modern tribalism, confirmation bias, self-censorship. So, all these create environment where a person only encounters information or opinions that reflects their own.

Internet media: Many websites provide different information with varied configurations of communication in the form of text, audio, and video. Websites or social network apps with webcasting, electronic publishing or any exhibition or display of authentic material over the internet could be few types of internets media. some of the websites or social media apps could be Yahoo, Bing, Google, Facebook, YouTube, LinkedIn, Instagram etc., initially it had reduced echo chambers as different opinions flourished across these internet networks. With time people started using digital tools and search engines to find content that aligns to their worldview or cultures, thus creating echo chambers.

Filter Bubbles: Digital tools allows users to filter out content or information that user does not find interesting, is also viewed as echo chamber. A filter bubble causes user to get significantly less contact with contradicting viewpoints, the personalized searches cause the user to become intellectually isolated. Personalised search results.

Broadcast media: broadcast media is information streamed electronically through signals, it includes television, radio, video games, audio recording, any form of movie or film, any materials supplied by the media and press, websites, online streaming, blogs and podcasts. whole nation gets information through dominated few broadcast medias. For example, well known television network can villainize someone accused of wrongdoing without any consideration of the evidence.

Modern tribalism: Modern tribalism refers to the phenomenon of people forming groups based on shared characteristics such as ethnicity, religion, political affiliation or other identity markers. These groups often create an "us vs. them" mentality, which can lead to polarization and conflict between different groups. Modern tribalism can have both positive and negative effects. On the one hand, it can provide a sense of belonging and community for people who may feel isolated or marginalized in society. On the other hand, it can also lead to intolerance, discrimination, and violence towards those who are seen as outsiders or enemies.

Overall, modern tribalism is a complex and multifaceted phenomenon that reflects the human tendency to form groups and seek social connections. Understanding its causes and consequences is important for building a more inclusive and harmonious society.

Confirmation bias: Confirmation bias is the tendency for people to seek out and interpret information in a way that confirms their existing beliefs or hypotheses, while ignoring or dismissing information that contradicts them. This bias can lead to errors in judgment and decision-making, as well as reinforcing pre-existing beliefs and stereotypes.

For example, if someone believes that a particular medical treatment is effective, they may be more likely to seek out information that supports their belief and ignore information that suggests the treatment may not be effective or may have negative side effects. Similarly, if someone has a pre-existing political belief, they may be more likely to accept news sources and information that align with their beliefs and dismiss sources that contradict their views.

Confirmation bias can occur unconsciously, as people tend to seek out information that confirms what they already believe, while ignoring or dismissing information that challenges their beliefs. This can lead to a narrowing of perspective and an inability to consider alternative viewpoints.

Self-censorship: Self-censorship refers to the act of suppressing or withholding one's own thoughts, beliefs, or behaviors in order to conform to societal norms or avoid potential negative consequences such as criticism, rejection, or punishment.

Self-censorship can be conscious or unconscious and can manifest in various ways, such as refraining from expressing one's opinions in public, avoiding certain topics of conversation, or altering one's behavior to fit in with a particular group. Self-censorship can also occur in response to perceived threats, such as fear of being ostracized or persecuted for one's beliefs.

Self-censorship can have both positive and negative effects. On the positive side, it can help maintain social order and prevent conflict by encouraging people to adhere to societal norms and avoid offending others. On the negative side, self-censorship can stifle creativity, impede open communication, and limit the diversity of ideas and perspectives within a society. It can also contribute to the perpetuation of social injustices and discrimination by discouraging dissenting voices and alternative viewpoints.

Reducing self-censorship requires creating a culture that values free expression and encourages respectful dialogue, even when opinions differ. It also involves creating safe spaces where people feel comfortable expressing themselves without fear of retribution. Finally, it involves encouraging individuals to develop a strong sense of self and the confidence to express their beliefs and opinions, even in the face of potential criticism or rejection.

Chapter – 2

Industry Reports and Studies

The number of social media users worldwide continued to grow in 2023, latest figures in the year 2023 are expected to be over 4.89 billion users worldwide and is forecasted over 5.8 billion social media users worldwide by 2027. Facebook, the biggest social media platform has 2.9 billion users as of 2023. Most of the frequent users of social media apps are Millennial's and Gen Z, more than

80% of worlds 5 billion users access apps through mobile phones. United States holds third spot in the world with 302 million social media users of which 85% of Americans use smart phones.

India ranks second with more than 500 million social media users. China with 1.02 billion users is the country with most social media user in 2023.

Social media trends in 2023 are User-Generated Content (UGC), Micro-influencers, short-form videos, and live streaming. TikTok is the fastest growing social media platform with more than a billion users.

As of January 2023, 64% of world's total population use the internet, which is 5.16 billion people who have access to internet. Latest statistics indicates that 100 million internet users grew in one year as of January 2023. With of 7.8 billion of total world population number of unconnected to internet has fallen to 2.64 billion, with majority of people living in Africa and Asia. It is predicted that two-thirds of the world's population should be online by the end of 2023.

Some of the social media applications that were launched in order are:

1. Friendster started on March 22, 2002

2. LinkedIn was launched on May 5, 2003

3. Myspace launched on August 2003

4.   Orkut launched on January 22, 2004

5.   Flickr launched on February 10, 2004

6.   Hi5 launched on June 27, 2004

7.   Facebook launched on Feb 4, 2004

8.   YouTube launched on Feb 14, 2005

9.   Reddit launched on June 23, 2005

10.   Twitter launched on March 21, 2006

11.   Tumblr launched on Feb 2007

12.   WhatsApp launched on Jan 2009

13.   Weibo launched on Aug 14, 2009

14.   Instagram launched on Oct 6, 2010

15.   Google Plus app launched on June 28,

2011

Friendster was one of the first social networks which was launched in 2002, preceding myspace, Facebook, Twitter, YouTube, and LinkedIn. In the year 2009 YouTube had many users followed by Facebook, 2010 Facebook took over the market.

Source: https://datareportal.com/social-media-users

Kepios is a strategy consulting company that helps organisations worldwide to make sense of peoples evolving digital behaviours. So, a detailed analysis and report by Kepios team shows that there are 4.76 billion social media users worldwide in January 2023, equating to 59.4% of total global population. With an average of 137 million new users joining social media every 12 months. This growth shows an annualised growth of 3 % where we have more than 4 users every single second.

Latest figure shows that 9 out of 10 internet users now use social media each month. These are

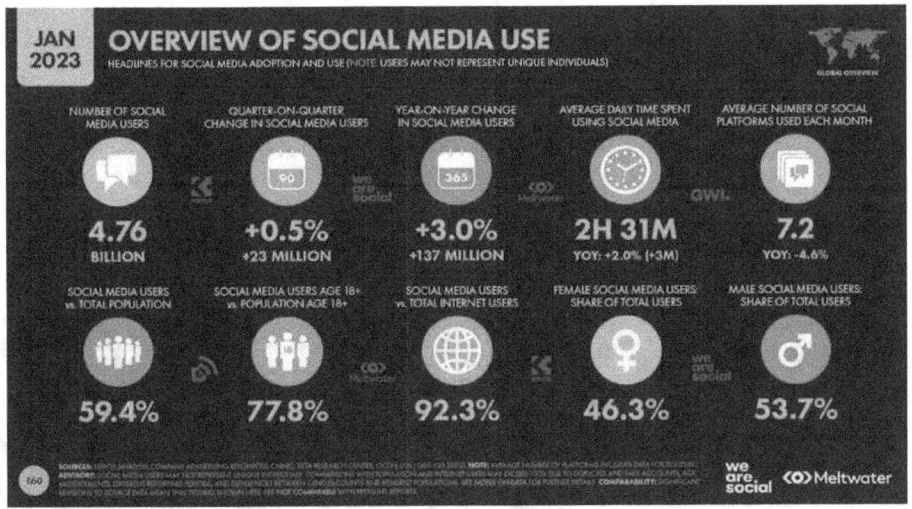

approximate numbers as there could be issues of duplicate accounts.

There are six social media platforms that claim one billion monthly active users. Three of these six platforms is owned by Meta. Facebook is still the world's most widely used social media platform with 2.9 billion monthly active users. YouTube is

supposed to have 2.5 billion active users and

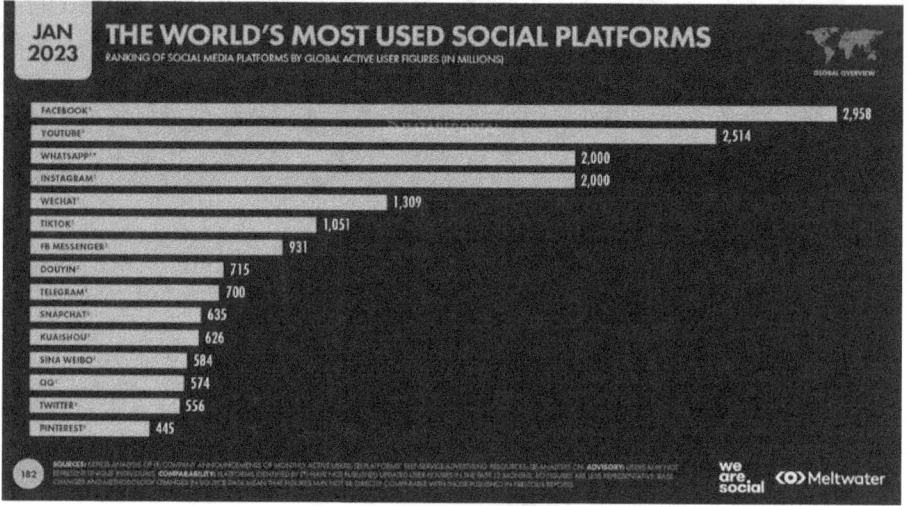

Source: https://datareportal.com/social-media-users

WhatsApp and Instagram have at least 2 billion

monthly active users. TikTok and WeChat has

approximately 1 billion to 1.5 billion monthly active

users. Telegram has 700 million monthly users,

Snapchat has 635 million monthly users and Twitter's potential advertising reach is roughly 556 million.

Industry Report for 2022:

According to industry reports and studies, the following were some of the key social media statistics in 2022:

1. User base: The number of social media users worldwide continued to grow in 2022, reaching over 4 billion users.

2. Popular platforms: The most popular social media platforms in 2022 included Facebook, YouTube, WhatsApp, WeChat, and Instagram.

3. Time spent: The average person spent over 2 hours per day on social media in 2022.

4. Advertising revenue: Social media platforms generated billions of dollars in advertising revenue in 2022, with Facebook and Google being the largest players in the market.

5. Video content: Video content became increasingly popular on social media in 2022, with platforms like TikTok and Instagram leading the way in terms of user engagement.

6. E-commerce: Social media platforms continued to expand their e-commerce capabilities in 2022, allowing businesses to

reach consumers directly through shoppable posts and other features.

7. Privacy concerns: Concerns about privacy and data protection on social media remained high in 2022, with regulators and users calling for greater transparency and accountability from tech companies.

These statistics highlight the continued growth and influence of social media in 2022, as well as some of the challenges faced by the industry and its users.

Industry Reports 2023:

Social media has become an integral part of our daily lives and its usage is expected to continue growing in the coming years. Here are some potential social media statistics for 2023 based on current trends:

1. Increased usage of social media: Social media usage is expected to continue to increase, especially in emerging markets. According to a report by Hootsuite and We Are Social, as of January 2021, there were 4.20 billion active social media users worldwide, with a growth

rate of 13.2% year-over-year. This trend is expected to continue in 2023.

2. Mobile usage continues to dominate: The majority of social media users access their accounts through mobile devices. This trend is expected to continue, with mobile usage accounting for more than 90% of social media usage in 2023.

3. Video content will continue to dominate: Video content has become increasingly popular on social media, with platforms like YouTube, TikTok, and Instagram Reels leading the way. In 2023, it's likely that video content will continue to dominate social media, with

live streaming and short-form video content becoming even more popular.

4. Social commerce will grow: Social commerce is the practice of selling products directly on social media platforms. This trend is expected to continue to grow in 2023, as more businesses look to sell their products directly to consumers through social media.

5. Influencer marketing will continue to be popular: Influencer marketing has become a popular way for brands to reach their target audience on social media. In 2023, it's likely that influencer marketing will continue to be popular, with more businesses partnering

with influencers to promote their products and services.

Overall, social media usage is expected to continue growing in 2023, with a continued focus on mobile usage, video content, social commerce, and influencer marketing.

Chapter – 3

Social Media and Mental Health

Social media can have a detrimental effect on mental health and well-being, causing feeling of anxiety, loneliness, and low self-esteem, while multiple studies referenced by **The Child Mind Institute** and **The National Centre for Health Research** have found a strong link between social media and increased risk for depression, self-harm, and suicidal thoughts among youth, due to their negative experiences such as inadequacy about their life and appearance.

Social media is almost addictive, as when one opens some of the apps and see the content it gives some people high pleasure by releasing dopamine, which is a chemical linked to happiness and pleasurable activities such as consuming good food, drugs or sex. Once someone get addicted to social media, there is a lot of emphasis on interactions or responses one receives on the content shared on social media app, content which could be a picture or an article. When the content does not get the feedback one desires or is invalidated or disappointing, then the user experiences disappointment, low self-esteem, anxiety or even depression.

Filters on social media exemplifies how social media apps can be both positive and negative. There are filters for fun where you can have a great laugh and these fun tools are entertainer keeping lot of them in good moods. Experts say that there is direct link between social media filters and low self-esteem, self-confidence, and higher cases of body or muscle dysmorphia. Filters are available on most social media apps like Instagram, Facebook, Snapchat etc.

Spending too much time on these filters can harm the users by altering their real appearances and setting higher expectations about their appearances. So as a result, users are dissatisfied with their real appearance compared to the altered selves with the beauty filters.

Body dysmorphia (BDD) is a mental health condition where a person is worried about flaws in their appearance, people of any age can have BDS, but its more common among youth, teenagers, and young adults. Muscle dysmorphia (MD) is a subtype of BDD, being preoccupied by worries that one's body is too small or not muscular enough. Some of the negative impacts of BDD that the parents should watch out for their children behaviour like: Low Self-esteem, Major depression, Mood disorders, Anxiety disorder, Obsessive-compulsive disorder, Social Isolation, Eating disorder and Substance misuse.

Social media anxiety disorder is a condition that can develop when social media use causes excessive and persistent anxiety or distress. This anxiety can be related to a fear of missing out (FOMO), fear of negative social evaluation, or fear of social interaction in general.

Fear of Missing Out (FOMO): When messages and jokes are shared on social media among friends or classmates, some of them are worried about missing out on the information and connecting to their peers, if they do not regularly check their apps. So, this leads to constant checking and scrolling through the social media app having detrimental effect on studies. Having a whole digital world at fingertips can put a damper on having real social connections and in-person interactions.

University of Pennsylvania study suggests using less of social media can help have a positive mental health, decreasing depression and loneliness. One should recognise and be aware of these warning signs like:

- Spending more time on social media at the cost of schoolwork or studies.

- De-prioritizing or neglecting routine work, hobbies, and regular activities.

- Comparing self with others frequently and feeling low or jealous.

- Engaging in risky behaviours or posting outrageous pictures to gain likes and comments.

- Watch out for being trolled for posts shared.

- Noticing that your personal and social relationships are suffering.

People with social media anxiety disorder may feel the need to constantly check their social media accounts, be excessively preoccupied with likes and comments, or feel overwhelmed by the amount of information they are exposed to on social media platforms. This can lead to symptoms such as restlessness, irritability, difficulty concentrating, and sleep disturbances.

Social media anxiety disorder can be treated through a variety of methods, including cognitive-behavioral therapy (CBT), medication, and lifestyle changes. CBT can help individuals identify and challenge negative thoughts related to social media, while medication may be used to alleviate anxiety symptoms. Lifestyle changes, such as limiting social media use, engaging in activities that promote relaxation and self-care, and increasing face-to-face social interaction, can also be effective in managing social media anxiety disorder.

Just like FOMO "Facebook depression" is another term used, which can affect a person's mental health. The concept behind Facebook depression is that social media use can lead to feelings of social isolation, low self-esteem, and depression.

On social media platforms like Facebook, people are often presented with images and updates from others that can create an unrealistic portrayal of others' lives, leading to feelings of inadequacy or inferiority. Additionally, the constant comparison to others can cause people to feel left out or excluded from social events and activities, leading to further social isolation and negative emotions.

Research has shown that excessive social media use, including on Facebook, can be linked to higher rates of depression and anxiety in young people. However, it's important to note that social media use does not necessarily cause depression or anxiety, and many people use social media without experiencing negative effects.

To mitigate the potential negative effects of social media use, it's important to practice healthy habits, such as limiting time spent on social media, engaging in face-to-face social interaction, and focusing on positive relationships and experiences rather than comparison to others. Additionally, seeking professional help may be necessary if social media use is impacting mental health and well-being.

Digital detox is the solution for addiction by replacing the time with meeting people and having one-to-one conversations, spend time on hobbies or engaging with the community, best way to be mindful is:

- Determine a fixed time to browse or spend time on social media apps.

- Ask yourself the importance of spending your valuable time, unless it is used for constructivism, like you are using it for your positive development and growth or a part of your job, or you are being a positive social media contributor or building relationships for your business or a blogger.

- Keep a check on self and be disciplined, by practising this mindfulness will come a realisation that you have better and constructive ways to spend your time.

- Social media is a fantastic and great tool if used constructively.

Chapter 4

Pros and Cons of Social Media.

There is absolutely no excuse for ignorance in this age of information and digital world. Ignorance could be real threat to survival.

Positive effects:

1. Connectivity

2. Access to information

3. Opportunities to self-expression

4. Business and career opportunities.

Negative effects:

1. Mental health

2. Addiction

3. Spread of misinformation

4. Cyberbullying

5. Decreased attention span.

Overall, the impact of social media apps is complex and multifaceted, with both positive and negative effects. It is important for individuals to use these platforms responsibly and in moderation to maximise the positive effects and minimise the negative.

Social media allows people to communication easily and instantly with friends, family and even strangers from all over the world. Communication and connectivity can be a great tool for professional networking and job hunting. As per recent statistics 84% of organisations are recruiting through social media where 67% of employers use social media sites to research potential job candidates. 95% of recruiters use social media for recruitment, and 70% of managers globally have had success hiring through social media.

Around 97% of companies with more than 250 employees use it for recruiting employees. Glassdoor states that more than 75% of job seekers use social media when conducting their job search. 40 million people look for jobs on LinkedIn weekly. Most industries like marketing, hospitality, retail, consulting and information technology use social media for recruiting. Some of the Social media recruiting statistics from 2021, that may still be relevant and useful for reference are below:

1. According to a survey by Jobvite, 75% of recruiters use social media to evaluate

candidates, with LinkedIn being the most popular platform for recruitment.

2. Another survey by CareerArc found that 91% of employers use social media to screen job applicants, and 69% have rejected candidates based on their social media profiles.

3. A study by Hootsuite found that 48% of job seekers use social media in their job search, and 29% of job seekers have used social media to apply for a job.

4. The same Hootsuite study also found that the most popular social media platforms for job seekers are LinkedIn (92%), Facebook (42%), Twitter (34%), and Instagram (25%).

5. Video job ads on social media are becoming increasingly popular, with a survey by LinkedIn finding that 54% of recruiters have used video in their job ads.

6. Social media recruiting can lead to faster and more efficient hiring. A study by SHRM found that companies that use social media for recruitment have seen a 49% increase in candidate quality and a 43% decrease in time-to-hire.

It's important to note that these statistics are from 2021, and the landscape of social media recruiting is constantly changing. Employers and recruiters should stay up-to-date with the latest trends and best practices in social media recruiting to stay competitive in the job market.

Social media has created new opportunities for businesses and individuals to promote their products and services, and to connect with potential clients and employers.

Social media has helped solve many criminal cases and difficult situations in various ways, including:

1. Identifying suspects: Social media platforms such as Facebook, Twitter, and Instagram have been instrumental in identifying and

apprehending suspects in criminal cases. Often, photos or videos of suspects are shared on social media, which helps law enforcement agencies track them down.

2. Finding missing persons: Social media has helped find missing persons by spreading the word quickly and efficiently. Family members and friends can share information about the missing person on social media, and it can be shared and re-shared until it reaches a wider audience. In some cases, social media has been instrumental in locating missing persons alive and well.

3. Providing evidence: Social media posts can provide crucial evidence in criminal cases. For example, posts about drug use or criminal activity can be used as evidence in court. Social media posts have also been used to establish an alibi or prove someone's whereabouts at a particular time.

4. Crowd-sourcing information: Social media can be used to crowd-source information in cases where law enforcement agencies need public assistance. For example, after the Boston Marathon bombing in 2013, social media was used to help identify suspects by asking the

public to share any relevant information or photos.

Social media has been a valuable tool in solving criminal cases and difficult situations. However, it is important to note that social media can also be used to spread false information or harm the reputation of innocent people, so it should always be used responsibly and ethically.

In recent years, there have been number of high-profile cases involving social media apps that have had a significant impact on society and raise important questions about privacy, free speech, and the role of technology in our lives. My next article on cases involving social media worldwide

will be out soon, for your reference.

Chapter 5

Social Media and Youth.

Social media has become an integral part of our daily lives, and its impact on the youth has been a topic of discussion for many years. As we move into 2023, social media is expected to continue to have a significant influence on the youth, both positively and negatively.

On the positive side, social media has provided a platform for the youth to express themselves, connect with others, and access information on a variety of topics. It has also provided opportunities for education, entrepreneurship, and activism.

One of the most significant impacts of social media on the youth has been the democratization of information. With the click of a button, young people can access a wealth of information on a variety of topics, from news and politics to entertainment and pop culture. This has provided opportunities for self-education and growth, as well as increasing awareness about social issues.

Social media has also provided opportunities for young people to connect with others who share similar interests or experiences. Social media platforms like TikTok and Instagram have become hubs for communities of young people who are passionate about specific topics, such as fashion, makeup, or music. These communities can provide a sense of belonging and support that may be lacking in other areas of their lives.

On the negative side, social media has also been linked to a number of negative outcomes for young people, such as cyberbullying, addiction, and mental health issues. Young people may feel pressure to present a certain image of themselves online, leading to feelings of inadequacy and low self-esteem. Social media may also contribute to feelings of isolation and loneliness, as young people spend more time interacting with screens than with real people.

As we move into 2023, it will be important for young people to be mindful of their social media use and its potential impact on their mental health and wellbeing. Parents, educators, and policymakers will also need to work together to promote safe and responsible social media use among young people.

In conclusion, social media is likely to continue to have a significant impact on the youth in 2023. While it provides many opportunities for self-expression, connection, and learning, it also poses risks and challenges that need to be addressed. By promoting responsible social media use and supporting young people in navigating its complexities, we can help ensure that social media remains a positive force in their lives.

Chapter 6

Social Media and Marketing

Social media has transformed the way businesses market their products and services, and its impact is expected to continue in 2023. Here are some potential trends in social media marketing in 2023:

1. Increased use of video content: Video content has become increasingly popular on social media, and its usage is expected to continue

growing in 2023. Platforms like TikTok and Instagram Reels have seen significant growth in recent years, and businesses are expected to continue leveraging short-form video content to reach their target audience.

2. Personalization and customization: As social media algorithms become more sophisticated, businesses will need to focus on personalization and customization to stand out from the crowd. This may involve tailoring content to specific audiences or using social media listening tools to track consumer behavior and preferences.

3. Influencer marketing: Influencer marketing has become an increasingly popular way for businesses to reach their target audience on social media. In 2023, it's likely that influencer marketing will continue to be popular, with businesses partnering with influencers to promote their products and services.

4. Social commerce: Social commerce is the practice of selling products directly on social media platforms. This trend is expected to continue to grow in 2023, as more businesses look to sell their products directly to consumers through social media.

5. Augmented reality (AR) and virtual reality (VR): AR and VR technologies are becoming increasingly sophisticated, and businesses are expected to leverage them to enhance the customer experience on social media. For example, businesses may use AR filters to allow consumers to "try on" products virtually or use VR technology to create immersive brand experiences.

6. Social media advertising: Social media advertising has become an important part of many businesses' marketing strategies. In 2023, businesses are expected to continue to

invest in social media advertising to reach their target audience and drive conversions.

Overall, social media is expected to continue to be an important part of businesses' marketing strategies in 2023. By leveraging new technologies and focusing on personalization, customization, and engagement, businesses can create impactful social media campaigns that drive growth and connect with their target audience.

Chapter 7

Social Media and Personal Branding.

Personal branding has become increasingly important in the age of social media, and its impact is expected to continue to grow in 2023. Here are some potential trends in personal branding on social media in 2023:

1. Authenticity and transparency: As social media becomes more crowded, it will become

increasingly important for individuals to be authentic and transparent in their personal branding efforts. This may involve sharing personal stories or experiences, as well as being open and honest about successes and failures.

2. Micro-influencers: In 2023, micro-influencers are expected to become more important in personal branding efforts. These are individuals with smaller followings who have highly engaged audiences in niche areas. Working with micro-influencers can be an effective way to build a personal brand and reach a highly targeted audience.

3. Personalized content: Personalization will continue to be a key trend in personal branding on social media. This may involve tailoring content to specific audiences or using social media listening tools to track consumer behavior and preferences.

4. Diversification: In 2023, individuals will need to diversify their social media presence to stand out from the crowd. This may involve using different platforms for different purposes, such as using LinkedIn for professional networking and TikTok for creative expression.

5. Storytelling: Storytelling has become an important part of personal branding on social media, and this trend is expected to continue in 2023. Individuals will need to use storytelling techniques to create engaging and compelling content that resonates with their target audience.

6. Emphasis on personal values: In 2023, personal branding efforts will likely place an emphasis on personal values and beliefs. Individuals will need to communicate their values and beliefs through their social media presence to create a strong and authentic personal brand.

Personal branding on social media is expected to continue to be important in 2023. By focusing on authenticity, personalization, diversification, and storytelling, individuals can create a strong and impactful personal brand that resonates with their target audience.

Chapter 8

Social Media and Business.

Social media has given rise to entrepreneurs by providing new and innovative ways for individuals to reach and engage with potential customers, build their brand, and market their products or services. Here are some of the ways social media has contributed to the rise of entrepreneurs:

Low barrier to entry, where social media platforms such as Facebook, Instagram, and Twitter provide a low-cost and accessible way for entrepreneurs to connect with their target audience without the need for significant investment in traditional advertising or marketing.

Access to a wider audience is at the tip of their finger, social media allows entrepreneurs to reach a wider audience beyond their geographic location, allowing them to build a customer base and expand their business beyond their local area.

Building brand identity has become very easy and cost effective, social media platforms provide a way for entrepreneurs to build and establish their brand identity, communicate their values and mission, and differentiate themselves from their competitors.

Networking opportunities are much easier, social media allows entrepreneurs to connect with like-minded individuals, potential business partners, and industry experts, providing opportunities for collaboration and growth.

Customer feedback at a click, social media provides entrepreneurs with a platform to engage with their customers, gather feedback, and make necessary improvements to their products or services, leading to increased customer satisfaction and loyalty.

Social media has transformed the way businesses operate, and its impact is expected to continue to grow in 2023. Here are some potential trends in social media and business in 2023:

Increased use of chatbots: Chatbots are becoming increasingly sophisticated, and businesses are expected to leverage them to enhance customer service on social media. Chatbots can be used to quickly respond to customer inquiries, provide product recommendations, and assist with purchases.

Personalization and customization: As social media algorithms become more sophisticated, businesses will need to focus on personalization and customization to stand out from the crowd. This may involve tailoring content to specific audiences or using social media listening tools to track consumer behavior and preferences.

E-commerce integration: E-commerce integration is the practice of selling products directly on social media platforms. This trend is expected to continue to grow in 2023, as more businesses look to sell their products directly to consumers through social media.

Social media advertising: Social media advertising has become an important part of many businesses' marketing strategies. In 2023, businesses are expected to continue to invest in social media advertising to reach their target audience and drive conversions.

Influencer marketing: Influencer marketing has become an increasingly popular way for businesses to reach their target audience on social media. In 2023, it's likely that influencer marketing will continue to be popular, with businesses partnering with influencers to promote their products and services.

Social media analytics: Social media analytics tools are becoming more sophisticated, allowing businesses to gain valuable insights into consumer behavior and preferences. In 2023, businesses are expected to continue to use social media analytics to inform their marketing strategies and drive growth.

Social media is expected to continue to be an important part of businesses' operations in 2023. By leveraging new technologies and focusing on personalization, customization, and engagement, businesses can create impactful social media campaigns that drive growth and connect with their target audience.

Business Success Stories:

There are numerous success stories of new entrepreneurs who have leveraged social media to build successful businesses, let's have a look at few:

Warby Parker or JAND, Inc: Warby Parker is an online retailer of prescription glasses, contact lens and sunglasses, based in New York City. This online eyewear company was founded in 2010 by four friends who met at business school. The company was started in the venture initiation program of the *Wharton School of the University of Pennsylvania,* the company was able to scale quickly by leveraging social media to promote their brand and products. Today, Warby Parker is valued at over $1.35 billion.

Link: https://www.warbyparker.com/

Daniel Wellington: Daniel Wellington is a Swedish watch brand company that was founded in 2011 by Filip Tysander. Tysander leveraged Instagram influencers to promote his watches, and the brand quickly gained a following. Today, Daniel Wellington is worth over $200 million.

Link: https://www.danielwellington.com/us/

Gymshark: Gymshark is a British fitness apparel company that was founded in 2012 by Ben Francis. The company was able to build a massive following on using social media, from Instagram to YouTube and TikTok, to organically market its products by partnering with fitness influencers. Today, Gymshark is valued at over $1 billion.

Link: https://eu.gymshark.com/

Calm, Inc: Calm is a US based meditation and mental wellness app that was founded in 2012 by Michael Acton Smith and Alex Tew. The company leveraged social media to build awareness around their app, which includes guided meditations, sleep stories, and music for relaxation. Today, Calm is valued at over $2 billion.

Link: https://www.calm.com/

Fabletics, LLC : Fabletics is a US based fitness apparel company that was founded in 2013 by Kate Hudson. The company leveraged social media to build a community of engaged customers who helped spread the word about the brand. Today, Fabletics is valued at over $1 billion.

Link: https://www.fabletics.com/

Casper Sleep Inc: Casper is a US based mattress company that was founded in 2014 by five friends. The company was able to build a strong brand on social media by leveraging influencer partnerships and user-generated content. Today, Casper is valued at over $1 billion.

Link: https://casper.com/

Glossier: Glossier is a beauty company that was founded in 2014 by Emily Weiss. The company leveraged social media to build a community of engaged customers who helped spread the word about the brand. Today, Glossier is valued at over $1 billion.

Link: https://www.glossier.com/

Allbirds, Inc: Allbirds is a footwear company that was founded in 2016 by Tim Brown and Joey Zwillinger. The company was able to build a strong brand on social media by leveraging influencer partnerships and user-generated content. Today, Allbirds is valued at over $1.4 billion.

Link: https://www.allbirds.com/

Hims & Hers Health, Inc: Hims & Hers is a telemedicine company that was founded in 2017 by Andrew Dudum. The company leveraged social media to build awareness around their products and services, which include treatments for hair loss, acne, and sexual wellness. Today, Hims & Hers is valued at over $1 billion.

Link: https://www.forhims.com/

Link: https://www.forhers.com/

Kylie Cosmetics, LLC: Kylie Jenner is a social media sensation and a successful entrepreneur. She leveraged her massive Instagram following to launch her cosmetics line, Kylie Cosmetics. In 2019,

she sold a 51% stake in her company to Coty for

$600 million.

Link: https://kyliecosmetics.com/

Chapter 9

Social Media and Privacy.

Privacy concerns have become a major issue for social media users, and it's expected that this trend will continue in 2023. Here are some potential trends in social media and privacy in 2023:

In 2023, there will be an increased focus on data privacy, particularly as governments around the world begin to implement stricter regulations. Social media platforms will need to be transparent about how they collect and use user data, and provide users with more control over their personal information.

Social media platforms are expected to continue to offer more granular privacy settings to users, allowing them to control who can see their content and personal information. Users will be able to choose which information to share and with whom, and will be able to adjust their privacy settings based on their preferences.

Two-factor authentication (2FA) was commercially made available by the RSA company as a key fob in 1986, is expected to become a more common feature on social media platforms. 2FA and Multi-Factor Authentication (MFA) adds an extra layer of security to users' accounts by requiring them to provide a second form of authentication, such as a fingerprint, or a code sent to their email or phone, in addition to their password. In 2023, these methods would be replaced by highly sophisticated Multi-Factor Authentication (MFA)

Encryption is becoming increasingly important for social media users who want to ensure their conversations and personal information are secure. In 2023, social media platforms are expected to continue to improve their encryption technologies to protect users' data and conversations.

Transparency reports are a way for social media platforms to share information about how they handle user data with their users. In 2023, social media platforms are expected to provide more detailed transparency reports to help users understand how their data is being used.

Privacy concerns are expected to remain a major issue for social media users in 2023. Social media platforms will need to continue to improve their privacy features and be more transparent about how they handle user data to earn users' trust and

maintain their loyalty.

Chapter – 10

Conclusion

Here are some general pieces of advice that could be helpful for various groups regarding social media in 2023 and beyond:

1. Be aware of your digital footprint: Everything you post on social media can be traced back to you, so be mindful of the information you share. What you say and do on social media

can affect your reputation and even your job prospects in the future.

2. Practice digital citizenship: Be respectful of others online, just as you would be in person. This means refraining from cyberbullying, being aware of your tone and language, and not sharing inappropriate content.

3. Be critical of the content you consume: Not everything you see on social media is true, so be sure to fact-check before believing or sharing something. Don't believe everything you read or see on social media, and try to find reputable sources to verify any claims.

4. Be mindful of your mental health: Social media can be a great way to connect with others, but it can also be a source of stress and anxiety. Limit your screen time, take breaks when needed, and be aware of how social media affects your mood.

5. Protect your privacy: Be cautious when sharing personal information on social media, and adjust your privacy settings to limit who can see your posts and information. This includes not sharing sensitive information like your home address or phone number.

6. Use social media as a tool for positive change: Social media can be a powerful tool for

activism and creating positive change. Use your platform to raise awareness about important issues, and connect with others who share your values.

7. Educate yourself about social media: Stay up-to-date with the latest trends and features on social media, and educate yourself about how to use it safely and responsibly. There are plenty of resources available online to help you learn more about social media and its impact on society.

References:

https://simplicable.com/en/echo-chamber

https://www.lancastergeneralhealth.org/health-hub-home/2021/september/the-effects-of-social-media-on-mental-health

https://www.demandsage.com/social-media-users/

https://oosga.com/social-media/ind/

https://datareportal.com/global-digital-overview

https://everyonesocial.com/blog/social-recruiting-statistics/

https://blog.pagefreezer.com/4-cases-solved-social-media

https://influencermarketinghub.com/social-media-sites/

https://www.wordstream.com/blog/ws/2022/01/11/most-popular-social-media-platforms

https://influencermarketinghub.com/social-media-marketing-benchmark-report/#toc-2

https://www.wordstream.com/blog/ws/2022/01/11/most-popular-social-media-platforms

https://www.seegerweiss.com/social-media-youth-harm?gclid=Cj0KCQjwvZCZBhCiARIsAPXbaju7CRA2Iijqaot7fP54kMh2mYUIt850AwQkezWfoCxjRzmYSfl0gH8aAuxQEALw_wcB

https://www.pewresearch.org/internet/2022/08/10/teens-social-media-and-technology-2022/
https://statusbrew.com/insights/social-media-statistics/

https://startupbonsai.com/social-media-statistics/
https://www.zippia.com/advice/social-media-statistics/

https://www.businessofapps.com/data/tiktok-report/?utm_source=tiktok&utm_medium=click&utm_campaign=featured-data-ad

https://www.businessofapps.com/data/social-app-report/

https://uploads3.craft.co/uploads/craft/source/document/18740/c7033e6ae7754f5e.pdf

https://www.businessofapps.com/data/report-app-data/

https://www.businessofapps.com/data/dating-app-report/

https://www.businessofapps.com/data/food-delivery-app-report/

https://www.businessofapps.com/data/apple-report/

https://www.businessofapps.com/data/instagram-report/

https://summitpsnews.org/2020/03/24/social-media-has-changed-the-lives-of-modern-society/

https://www.singlegrain.com/social-media/8-social-media-success-stories-to-inspire-you/

https://www.mcleanhospital.org/essential/it-or-not-social-medias-affecting-your-mental-health

https://www.ncbi.nlm.nih.gov/pmc/articles/PMC4183915/

https://www.nami.org/Your-Journey/Kids-Teens-and-Young-Adults/Teens/Social-Media-and-Mental-Health

https://www.medicalnewstoday.com/articles/social-media-and-mental-health

https://www.lancastergeneralhealth.org/health-hub-home/2021/september/the-effects-of-social-media-on-mental-health

https://datareportal.com/social-media-users#:~:text=Analysis%20from%20Kepios%20shows%20that,since%20this%20time%20last%20year.